ThinkBetter
LiveBetter

A Victorious Life Begins
in Your Mind

ThinkBetter
LiveBetter

STUDY GUIDE

A Victorious Life Begins
in Your Mind

Joel Osteen

Faith
Words

New York • Boston • Nashville

FaithWords
Hachette Book Group
1290 Avenue of the Americas
New York, NY 10104
faithwords.com
twitter.com/faithwords

First Edition: October 2016

FaithWords is a division of Hachette Book Group, Inc.
The FaithWords name and logo are trademarks of Hachette Book Group, Inc.

The publisher is not responsible for websites (or their content) that are not owned by the publisher.

The Hachette Speakers Bureau provides a wide range of authors for speaking events. To find out more, go to www.hachettespeakersbureau.com or call (866) 376-6591.

Literary development: Lance Wubbels Literary Services, Bloomington, Minnesota.

ISBN: 978-1-4555-9587-7

Printed in the United States of America

10 9 8 7 6 5 4 3 2 1

Contents

Introduction

We are delighted that you have chosen to use this study guide that was written as a companion to *Think Better, Live Better*. Your mind has incredible power over your success or failure. This study is meant to help you establish a simple yet life-changing strategy for erasing the thoughts that keep you down and reprogramming your mind with positive thinking to reach a new level of victory in every area of your life.

As a child of the Most High God, you are equipped to handle anything that comes your way. To claim your destiny, you need to start thinking about yourself the way God does and to delete the thoughts that tear down your confidence. The thoughts and questions addressed in the following pages will help you to train yourself to tune out the negativity and to tune into your calling, so you may begin to live the wonderful plans God has made for you.

How you use this study guide will depend on the purpose you have in mind. You can work through it on your own for personal development, as a part of a small group study or discussion, say in a care group or book club setting, or even during a weekend retreat.

The format of each chapter is simple and user-friendly. For maximum benefit, it is best to first read the corresponding chapter from *Think Better, Live Better*, and then work your way through the chapter in this study guide. The majority of the questions are personal, and taking the time to read through the chapters in the book and think through how each question can affect your life will give the study immediate personal application.

If you decide to use this study guide in a small group study, the most effective way is to go through each chapter on your own as preparation before each meeting. Take some time to read the relevant portions of text and to reflect on the questions and how they apply to you. This will give your group study depth and make the sessions more productive for all.

Because most of the questions are personal, if you use this study guide in a group setting or on a retreat, remember that courtesy and mutual respect lay the foundation for a healthy group. A small group should be a safe place for all who participate. Some of what will be shared is highly sensitive in nature and some may be controversial, so respect the confidentiality of the person who is sharing. Don't let your conversations leave the small group or turn into gossip. A small group is not a place to tell others what they should have done or said or think, and it's not a place to force opinions on others. Commit yourselves to listening in love to one another, to praying for and supporting one another, to being sensitive to their perspectives, and to showing each participant the grace you would like to receive from others.

CHAPTER ONE

Reprogram Your Mind

Similar to the making of a computer, when God created you, He put in you the perfect hardware. You're the right size, the right nationality, and you have the right gifts. He also put the right software in you. From the very beginning, your original software says, "You can do all things through Christ." He programmed, "Whatever you touch will prosper and succeed" and "You are a victor and not a victim." Your Creator designed you to live an abundant, victorious, faith-filled life.

We don't always experience this abundant life because we've allowed viruses to contaminate our software. We say to ourselves, "I'll never be successful." "I'll never break this addiction." "I'm just average." Because our software is infected, we're negative, don't believe our dreams will come to pass, and don't expect problems to turn around.

1. What was your immediate response to the statement that God programmed you to be victorious, healthy, strong, and creative? In what ways do you recognize that as true in your life, and in what ways would you say that viruses have infected your software?

> *If your thinking is limited, your life will be limited.*

To restore our original software, we need to learn to hit the delete button. When negative, discouraging thoughts come trying to contaminate your software, just hit delete before they start affecting how you live. Those thoughts that say, *You'll never get well. You'll never accomplish your dreams,* are viruses trying to keep you from your destiny. Delete them. Say to yourself, "My software says, 'God is restoring health back to me. I have the favor of God. Whatever I touch prospers and succeeds.'"

2. What thoughts do you have that you can identify as viruses that are having a negative effect on the way you live your life?

....

....

....

....

....

....

....

3. The good news is that you can restore your original software by dwelling on what your Creator says about you. What has God said about you in His Word that deletes the above negative thoughts?

....

....

....

....

....

....

....

The Scripture tells us to guard our heart and mind (see Prov. 4:23; Phil. 4:7), because the thoughts we dwell on control our whole life. You control the doorway to what you allow in. You can dwell on negative thoughts and derogatory comments, or you can choose to delete them and dwell on what God says about you.

4. On a scale of 1 to 10, with 1 being almost never and 10 being a consistent hitting of the delete button to negative thoughts, how would you rate your guarding of your mind? What do you base that score upon?

....

....

....

....

....

5. What negative comments have people said about you that you need to delete? How have those statements impacted your life?

....

....

....

....

....

....

....

*You are not
who people say
you are.*

Research shows that when children are bullied in school, the effects from bullies' negative, derogatory words, such as "loser" and "ugly" and "stupid," can often impact children's lives for years.

6. Were you bullied as a child? What was said to you that left an impact upon you?

    ....

    ....

    ....

    ....

7. Words spoken to you are seeds planted in your soil that only take root if you water them. How do you water them?

    ....

    ....

    ....

    ....

The Lord told Joshua, "Meditate on [the Word of God] day and night, so that you may be careful to do everything written in it. Then you will be prosperous and successful" (Josh. 1:8). When your mind is filled with thoughts of faith, hope, and victory, that's what will become a reality.

8. What thoughts do you fill your mind with? How can you find more ways to fill it with God's Word?

    ....

    ....

    ....

    ....

The story of the man who was raised by a very negative father who always put him down is tragic but not uncommon. That young man was angry and felt inferior, and all that negativity became a stronghold in his life that held him back until he discovered our Heavenly Father's blessing on his life and truths that reprogrammed his mind.

9. What words about who you are and what you can become did you receive as a child from your parents? How has that impacted you?

....

....

....

....

....

....

....

10. Maybe you are like the man in this story and you didn't receive your earthly father's or mother's blessing. The good news is that you have your Heavenly Father's blessing. What is He saying about you?

....

....

....

....

....

....

The lady who grew up feeling that she was never good enough and never fit in lived with insecurities that stemmed from being a child born out of wedlock. The word *illegitimate* became ingrained in her thinking. "You're a mistake. Nobody even wanted you. You're not valuable." She believed the lies, which dramatically affected her personality, her attitude, and even her marriage.

11. What did she discover about where our worth and value come from, and what difference has that made in her life?

....

....

....

....

....

....

The real battle is taking place in your mind. If you're defeated in your thoughts, you've already lost. You have to get rid of the viruses if you want to live better.

12. Pay close attention to what you're thinking. Are there any strongholds in your mind that are keeping you back? If so, name them. What thoughts can you use to break their hold?

> "Not only am I who God says I am, but I can do what God says I can do."

....

....

....

....

....

....

Little children start off so excited about life. They have big dreams. They're not intimidated or insecure. They believe they can do anything. Their thinking has not been contaminated. But over time, somebody tells them what they *can't* become, what they *can't* do. Little by little their self-esteem goes down. Negative thoughts begin to reprogram and distort their thinking about who they really are. Before long, they think, *I'll never do anything great. I'm not that talented. I'm just average.*

13. Do you find yourself living with excitement and expectation about your life and future? How has your thinking changed over the years?

....

....

....

....

....

....

14. What have you copied that you saw modeled when you were growing up that are wrong mind-sets that you need to start reprogramming?

....

....

....

....

....

....

My father grew up during the Great Depression with no money, a poor education, and no future to speak of. He had been programmed with poverty, defeat, and mediocrity. But when he gave his life to Christ, deep down, something said, "You were made for more than this." His attitude was, *This may be where I am, but this is not who I am. I may be in defeat, but I am not defeated. I'm a child of the Most High God.*

15. My father reprogrammed his thinking with thoughts of faith, hope, and victory. How can you do the same in those areas of your life where deep down you sense you were made for more?

....

....

....

....

....

....

16. You may have been raised in an environment filled with strife, addictions, conflict, low self-esteem, and mediocrity. What thoughts can you use to keep these negatives from setting the limits for your life?

....

....

....

....

....

....

When Carl Lewis was training for the Olympic Games, the experts said that according to their data, no person could jump over thirty feet. Carl Lewis responded by saying, "Yes, I know the experts say it can't be done, but I don't listen to that kind of talk. Thoughts like that have a way of sinking into your feet." Later that same year he went on to jump over thirty feet and break the world record.

17. Have negative thoughts sunk into your feet, stifling your potential and handicapping your life's race? How can adopting Lewis's attitude help you to break free from whatever is holding you down?

> *This is a new day. Strongholds are coming down. Get ready for God to do something new.*

18. Based on what you've learned in this chapter about what your Creator says about you, list three specific thoughts that you will use to reprogram your mind and clear out old viruses.

    1.

    2.

    3.

CHAPTER TWO

Remove Negative Labels

As a teenager, Walt Disney was told by a newspaper editor that he wasn't creative. Lucille Ball was told that she didn't have any acting skills. Winston Churchill was not thought of as a good student and twice failed the entrance examination into the Royal Military College Sandhurst. The common denominator in the success of these people is that they chose to remove the negative labels. Because they thought better than what others said, they lived far better than the labels had read.

1. People constantly put labels on us, telling us what we can and cannot become, what we do or don't have. How have you been labelled?

2. Have you allowed those labels to stick, or have you removed them?

People don't determine our destiny; God does.

When my father went to be with the Lord in 1999, I stepped up to pastor the church. I had never ministered before. One Sunday, after the service, I overheard two ladies talking in the lobby. One said, "Joel's not as good as his father." The other answered back, "Yes, I don't think the church is going to last." I was already insecure. I already felt unqualified, and *boom*, another negative label was stuck on me.

3. "Not good enough. Not up to par. Inferior." Why does the enemy love to put labels on you? How do the labels affect your thinking?

....

....

....

....

....

....

Removing labels is like peeling off an old car bumper sticker. You peel it, and it tears. You have to keep fighting those thoughts day after day. Finally, I removed that negative label, and I put on a new label: "I can do all things through Christ. I am strong in the Lord. I am anointed."

4. Are you still wearing a negative label that someone stuck on you? What label from God can you put on to replace it?

....

....

....

....

....

....

"Slow learner"—*I'll never be successful.* "Divorced"—*I'll never meet anyone new.* "Overweight"—*I'll never get in shape.* "Addicted"—*I'll never break these bad habits.* Whatever label you're wearing, you're going to become what that label says. You're giving that thought the power to shape and control how you live.

5. For thirty years, the one man floundered through life, having believed his junior high teacher was right in labelling him a "slow learner." What did he do to finally remove that label?

> *Don't let negative labels hold you back.*

_____

_____

_____

_____

_____

_____

Have you ever thought that the same God who can help you get by in life can help you excel in life? Why don't you remove those negative labels?

6. The real battle over removing negative labels takes place in your mind. Describe the battle that goes on in your mind.

_____

_____

_____

_____

_____

_____

_____

You serve a supernatural God. He can do what medicine cannot do. He is not limited by your education, your background, or the family you come from. He's not shaken by the things people have spoken over you. He's not up in Heaven frantically trying to figure out how to get you to your destiny. He knows the end from the beginning. He already has solutions to problems you've not even had yet. He is all-powerful and all-knowing.

7. Who put the negative labels on you? How does their knowledge and wisdom compare to our Creator's? Why give them the time of day?

....

....

....

....

....

....

To remove the old negative labels, all God asks of you is to believe what He says about you. When you believe, all things are possible.

8. What truth that God has spoken about you in His Word is He asking you to believe? What doors does He want to open for you that might not otherwise open?

....

....

....

....

....

....

In Joshua 6, we read that when the Israelites conquered the city of Jericho, the only people spared were the ones in the home of Rahab, a prostitute who had previously hid the spies from the king.

9. What labels do you think people had stuck on Rahab?

....

....

....

10. Of all the people God could have used to protect His people, He chose the prostitute Rahab. What does that say about how God views people's labels?

....

....

....

....

Rahab went on to marry a Jewish man named Salmon, and they had a son named Boaz, whose great grandson was King David. This means that Rahab, a former prostitute, is in the family line of Jesus Christ.

11. What does that say about the amazing way God can change any label that has been stuck on a person?

....

....

....

....

....

....

When I was growing up, I was very small. I grew six inches *after* high school. Somehow I got the nickname "Peanut." Everywhere I went, that's all I heard. "Hey, Peanut!" Every time I heard it, I was reminded that I was "below average, not up to par." I let that label stick, and I became less and less outgoing, quieter, more reserved. I finally pulled off that label when I realized that God made me just as I am on purpose.

12. God says you are a masterpiece. How would your life change if you put your shoulders back, held your head high, and wore this label proudly: "Child of the Most High God"?

....

....

....

....

....

....

....

13. One label that far too many people wear is the label "average." Do you say, "I'm just ordinary. I'm nothing special"? How does the fact that the Creator of the universe has breathed His life into you change that?

....

....

....

....

> *The truth is, there is nothing ordinary about you.*

....

....

In 1 Samuel 16, when the prophet Samuel came to anoint one of Jesse's sons to be the next king of Israel, Jesse didn't even bother to bring his youngest son, David, in from the fields. David's father seemed to have labeled David as "too small," "too young," "not very talented," and "not as smart as his brothers."

14. People usually look on the outside and label us. Where does God look when He labels us?

....

....

....

....

15. What do you think God sees in you that no one else can see?

....

....

....

....

16. Even after David had been anointed as the next king of Israel, his brother continued to stick negative labels on him. What gave David the strength to remove those labels and put on God's label instead?

....

....

....

....

The prophet Isaiah said, "No weapon forged against you will prevail, and you will refute every tongue that accuses you" (Isa. 54:17). That includes every negative label spoken over you. Notice, God is not going to do it. *You* have to show it to be in the wrong. In other words, you have to remove the negative label.

17. You have God's promise that nothing that's happened in your past has to keep you from your destiny. What was your first reaction when you read those words? How will you refute the negative labels?

_____

_____

_____

_____

_____

_____

18. As a teenager, Shaquille O'Neal was labelled as "Too big. Too slow. Too clumsy," yet he went on to become one of the greatest basketball players who ever played the game. What can we learn from his story about the labels that even the experts put on us?

_____

_____   *Experts built*
                                                    the Titanic,
_____   *and it sank.*

_____

_____

In Genesis 35, right before Jacob's wife Rachel died while giving birth to her second son, she named the boy Ben-oni, which means "son of my sorrow." She labeled him based on what she had experienced.

19. That negative label had nothing to do with the baby boy, but with the mother. What does that tell you about why people so often label others?

....

....

....

....

20. When Jacob heard the boy's name, he immediately said, "No, his name will be Benjamin," which means "son of strength, son of power, son of my right hand." What difference did that make in Benjamin's life?

....

....

....

....

21. Imagine that God is saying the same thing to you that He said to little Benjamin: "I am changing your name. I'm placing a new label on you." What would He call you?

....

....

....

....

CHAPTER THREE

Release the Full You

Inside each of us is a blessed, prosperous, victorious person who is free from addictions and bad habits, confident and secure, talented and creative. But just because this person is in you doesn't mean he or she is automatically going to come out. This person has to be released.

The apostle Paul gives us the secret in Romans 12:2: "Be transformed by the renewing of your mind." In the original language, the word *transformed* is *metamorphoo*. It's where we get our word for how caterpillars *metamorphose* into butterflies. If you'll program your mind with what God says about you, then a transformation will take place.

1. Compare the metamorphosis of the caterpillar to the process of change that must take place with our thoughts. What is the only way to release your butterfly?

....

....

....

....

> *God has predestined us to go through a transformation.*

....

....

....

....

....

2. What "wormy thoughts" do you have that will keep you in the cocoon and that need to be transformed?

....

....

....

....

....

....

....

....

....

3. When thoughts tell you what you can't be or what you can't do, what better thoughts can you tell yourself that will lead to the renewing of your mind?

....

....

....

....

....

....

....

....

....

....

....

Robert's story included the profound contrast in the influences of two stepfathers upon his life. His first stepfather always put him down, and his second stepfather constantly told Robert what he could become, how talented he was, and how there was a bright future in front of him.

4. When you read Robert's story, did people come to mind from your own experience who have had either a similar positive or negative impact on your life? How so?

   ....

   ....

   ....

   ....

   ....

   ....

   ....

5. Whether or not you have people in your life who call out your seeds of greatness, to reprogram your mind you need to find regular sources that speak faith to you and declare what God says you really are. Write a list of sources you can access daily as well as weekly.

   ....

   ....

   ....

   Your butterfly is waiting to soar! Release the full you.

   ....

   ....

   ....

When I first started ministering in 1999, I was so nervous. Every voice told me I couldn't do this. The enemy would have loved to keep me in my cocoon, thinking these wormy thoughts. He doesn't want you or me to break out and soar and live an overcoming life. He wants us to struggle in our mind, to be insecure, to be burdened by addictions and bad habits. If he can control our thoughts, he can control our whole life.

6. How did I break out of my cocoon, and how can you break out of yours?

    ....
    ....
    ....
    ....
    ....
    ....
    ....
    ....

7. What is the key to not getting discouraged as you make your way out of the cocoon and to getting rid of the wormy thoughts?

    ....
    ....
    ....
    ....
    ....
    ....
    ....

There was a man in Judges 6 named Gideon. Please read that chapter. God wanted him to lead the people of Israel against an opposing army, but Gideon had all these wormy thoughts. He was stuck in his cocoon.

8. What did the Angel of the Lord call Gideon? See Judges 6:12.

....

....

....

....

....

9. Describe Gideon's wormy thoughts in his response.

....

....

....

....

....

10. Just as Gideon had to do, where do you need to get in agreement with God and start believing what He says about you?

....

....

....

....

> *God didn't call Gideon what he was. He called him what he could become.*

....

....

In the story about the sculptor and the plantation owner, the sculptor takes what appeared to the owner as a worthless tree trunk and carved out a majestic soaring eagle that was so beautiful the owner stated he was willing to pay whatever price the sculptor wanted for it.

11. How could two people have such a different perspective on that tree trunk?

....

....

....

....

12. As you look upon your own life, would you say that you see what the sculptor would see or the plantation owner? Describe what you see.

....

....

....

....

....

....

13. If you see yourself as a tree trunk, what encouragement can you receive from the thought that your Creator is also your life Sculptor?

....

....

....

....

....

From the first time you see the man named Jacob in Genesis 25, you see that he was dishonest, a cheater and a deceiver. He even tricked his own brother out of his birthright as well as the blessing upon the firstborn son.

14. When you read about a deceiver such as Jacob, do you think of the worm or of the butterfly? Is a person with a lot of flaws someone beyond the hope of transformation?

....

....

....

....

....

....

....

15. Please read Genesis 32. Over the years, God kept working on Jacob, making him and molding him. What did God do to culminate the transformation of Jacob from a deceiver to "a prince"?

....

....

....

....

God will never give up on you.

....

....

....

....

....

One time in the Old Testament, an army invaded Jerusalem, kidnapped some of the people, and killed their king. The people of Israel were without a leader. They were discouraged and didn't know what to do. As they sat there thinking that it was over, the prophet Micah rose up and said, "Now why do you cry aloud? Is there no king in you?" (Mic. 4:9 ESV).

16. I believe God is saying the same thing to each of us: "There's a king in you." How does that change how you view yourself?

....

....

....

....

....

....

....

....

17. How can the king or the queen whom God has put in you be released?

....

....

....

....

....

....

....

....

Could it be that the only things holding you back from a better life are your thoughts toward yourself? You're focused on your mistakes, how you blew it, how you didn't measure up. You have to reprogram your thinking. Get rid of the wormy thoughts.

18. Gideon had his list of excuses and Jacob had his flawed character and failures that tried to hold them back from a better life. Today, what is your first thought as to what is trying to hold you back?

....

....

....

....

....

....

....

....

19. God didn't create you to crawl and squirm. He created you to soar. How can you get fully released from the cocoon?

....

....

....

....

....

Today is going to be the start of a transformation in your life!

....

....

....

CHAPTER FOUR

Think Yourself to Victory

Studies show that we talk to ourselves up to thirty thousand times a day. There is always something playing in our minds. The Scripture tells us to *meditate*, "to think about over and over," on God's promises. We need to pay attention to what we're meditating on.

Meditating is the same principle as worrying. When you worry, you're meditating on the wrong thing and using your faith in reverse. If you go through the day worried about your finances, family, and future, because you're allowing the wrong thoughts to play, it's going to cause you to be anxious, fearful, negative, and discouraged.

1. You control the doorway to your mind. When negative thoughts come knocking, how do you respond? What are the predominate thoughts that play on the screen of your mind throughout the day?

You have the power to say, "No, thanks," to any fearful, worrisome thoughts.

Philippians 4:8 says, "Whatever is true, whatever is noble, whatever is right, whatever is pure, whatever is lovely, whatever is admirable— if anything is excellent or praiseworthy—think about such things."

2. How do your thoughts throughout the day measure up to this standard? In what areas do you need to get your mind going in the right direction?

....

....

....

....

....

King David said, "Some trust in chariots and some in horses, but we trust in the name of the LORD our God" (Ps. 20:7). In modern times, he might say, "Some trust in their money, in their job, in what the economists say. But our trust is in Jehovah Jireh, the Lord our Provider."

3. When you think about your finances or career or future, how do your thoughts align with David's? How might meditating on this declaration of faith help you to live better?

....

....

....

....

....

....

Isaiah said about God, "You will keep in perfect peace those whose minds are steadfast, because they trust in you" (Isa. 26:3). If you keep your thoughts fixed on Him, He promises that you will have *perfect peace*!

4. What are you experiencing right now that is troubling and upsetting you? Does meditating on the problem make it better? How can changing the thoughts that you're dwelling on improve your peace of mind?

....

....

....

....

....

....

The apostle Paul said, "I think myself happy" (Acts 26:2 NKJV), even though it involved defending the gospel before King Agrippa, for which he was imprisoned and could die. Happiness starts in our thinking. Paul wasn't meditating on how bad it was. He was saying, "It may look bad, but my mind is filled with thoughts of hope, faith, and victory."

5. What was your immediate response to Paul's statement? What are some ways that you can think yourself happy and be at peace?

....

....

....

....

....

....

The Scripture tells us, "Arise [from spiritual depression to a new life], shine [be radiant with the glory and brilliance of the LORD]" (Isa. 60:1 AMP). The first place in which we have to arise is our thinking. Put on a new attitude with better thoughts. Purposefully think power thoughts.

6. Write a list of power thoughts that you will read out loud every day and meditate upon them.

....

....

....

....

....

....

....

Don't ever start the day in neutral or wait to see what kind of day it's going to be. You have to *decide* what kind of day it's going to be.

7. When you first get out of bed in the morning, what thoughts can you start with to set your mind in the right direction?

....

....

....

....

....

....

Jesus said to two blind men whom He healed, "Become what you believe" (Matt. 9:29 MSG). If you believe you'll never get out of debt, you probably won't. If you believe you're going to get laid off, don't be surprised if you do. Your faith is working.

8. Where in your life are you not becoming the person you want to be? What changes in your thinking will lead to the results you desire?

> *You are going to become what you believe.*

....

....

....

....

....

....

....

Job said, "The thing I greatly feared has come upon me" (Job 3:25 NKJV). Just as our faith can work in the right direction, it can work in the wrong direction.

9. Identify the areas of your thinking where you are most vulnerable to drawing in what is negative.

....

....

....

....

....

....

The Message Bible translation of Psalm 1 says that when you meditate on God's Word day and night, "you're a tree…bearing fresh fruit every month, never dropping a leaf, always in blossom." That's God's dream for your life—that even in the most difficult times, because you have your thoughts fixed on Him, you will know that God is still on the throne. He is fighting your battles, and you're not only going to come out, you're going to come out better off than you were before.

10. What does it mean to be in blossom when the health report is bad?

11. What does it mean to be in blossom when the economy goes down?

12. What does it mean to be in blossom when a relationship seems to have come to a hurtful end?

I've learned that if you fill your mind with the right thoughts, there won't be any room for the wrong thoughts. When you go around constantly thinking, *I'm strong. I'm healthy. I'm blessed. I have the favor of God*, then when the negative thoughts come knocking, there will be a "No Vacancy" sign. "Sorry, no room for you." They won't be able to get in.

13. Take some time now and consider your life as a house. Write an honest review of what occupies your rooms—fear or faith, lack or abundance, insecurity or confidence, "I can't" or "I can."

....

....

....

....

....

....

Before you go to bed at night, you lock the doors to your house to keep strangers out. Have that same thinking when it comes to your mind.

14. Write an announcement of "No Vacancy" in your mind for negative thoughts that want to come in and have a permanent home.

....

....

....

....

....

....

....

Once in the Scripture, Jesus was on His way to pray for a person who was very sick when people approached and said, "Tell Jesus it's too late. The person has already died." We are told that Jesus overheard but ignored the negative report (see Mark 5:36 AMPC). He didn't let it take root, meditate on it, or get discouraged and go back home. He also didn't deny that the report was true or pretend the person had not died. He knew that God had the final say, not people.

15. I'm not saying to deny the negative reports that are true and to act as though they don't exist, but describe a negative report in your life that you need to ignore what your thoughts are telling you. What do you need to affirm about it that God has the final say?

Don't let negative reports consume you to where that's all you think and talk about. Learn to put things in God's perspective.

As was true for the field goal kicker, in your life there will be times when it feels as though every voice is telling you, "You can't do it. It's not going to work out. You'll never overcome this problem." It may be the voices of the people around you, or it may just be voices in your mind, thoughts trying to discourage you. Don't be surprised if the enemy even starts replaying your failures and all your disappointments.

16. How did the field goal kicker overcome the overwhelming pressure to win the game? What did he tell himself?

....

....

....

....

....

....

17. Where is the first place we win the victory in any area of our life? Write a declaration that you will overcome and win the victory.

....

....

....

....

....

....

....

....

....

CHAPTER FIVE

Pregnant with Possibility

During the first few months of a pregnancy, a woman shows no sign that she's going to have a baby. But what you can't see is that on the inside a seed has taken root. Conception has occurred. Later, she'll start gaining weight, then she'll feel something kicking on the inside. She's still never seen the baby in person, but she knows the baby is on the way. Nine months after she conceives, she'll give birth to that baby.

In a similar way, you may not realize it, but you are pregnant. God has placed all kinds of potential in you—gifts, talents, and ideas. He's put dreams, businesses, books, songs, healing, and freedom inside you. You are pregnant with possibilities, with increase, with healing. The seed God put in you has already taken root. Just because you don't see anything happening doesn't mean it's not going to come to pass.

1. Write an honest review of what you believe God has placed inside you. What is He bringing to birth in and through your life?

....

....

....

....

....

....

....

....

Psalm 7:17 NLT reflects this principle: "The wicked…are pregnant with trouble and give birth to lies." The good news is: That's not you. You are the righteous. You're not pregnant with trouble, with bad breaks, or lack. You are pregnant with favor, with talent, with victory.

2. At what stage would you say you are at in your pregnancy? Do you see signs that it is coming to pass?

....

....

....

....

....

....

3. Instead of being discouraged and thinking, *This pregnancy is never going to happen. It's been so long. I've been through too much,* what attitude of expectancy should you cultivate to help you through it?

> *Know that what God started He will finish.*

....

....

....

....

....

....

....

....

....

PREGNANT WITH POSSIBILITY   47

4. Based upon the example of the man who was diagnosed with
    a very invasive type of cancer, write an outline on how you can
    take the principle of being pregnant and apply it to a medical
    report that doesn't look good, or to a debt, or to an addiction,
    or to a relationship problem. If possible, use a situation that
    you may be struggling with now.

    ....

    ....

    ....

    ....

    ....

    ....   *Don't go around*
                                                                                negative and
    ....   *complaining*
                                                                                about your
    ....   *situation. Turn*
                                                                                it around with
    ....   *better thoughts.*

    ....

    ....

    ....

    ....

    ....

    ....

    ....

    ....

    ....

    ....

In the Scripture, Sarah was over ninety years old when she gave birth to Isaac. This is way too old in the natural, but we serve a supernatural God. He can make a way where you don't see a way. Don't abort your baby. Don't give up on what God promised you. You can still give birth. You can still meet the right person, still start your own business, still go to college, still break the addiction. That seed is alive in you.

5. What did all of Sarah's outward circumstances tell her?

....

....

....

....

....

6. What do your outward circumstances tell you about the chances of your giving birth to your dreams?

....

....

....

....

....

7. How are you to view your outward circumstances as regards to what God put in you and is bringing to birth?

....

....

....

....

....

Statistics during the Great Depression said that given his limited environment, my father would have to stay on the farm and pick cotton the rest of his life. But Daddy told me, "Joel, when I was seventeen years old, I made the decision that my children would never be raised in the poverty and lack that I was raised in." What happened? He became pregnant. He could feel that baby kicking on the inside.

8. At that time, if someone were to have studied my father in his limited environment, they might have said that there was nothing special about him. What had already occurred in my father that would defy the statistics?

    ....

    ....

    ....

    ....

Statistics don't determine your destiny; God does. Where you are is not who you are.

    ....

    ....

    ....

9. Are there statistics that are stacked against you ever giving birth to what God has placed inside you? Describe them. How can you defy those statistics?

    ....

    ....

    ....

    ....

    ....

    ....

    ....

Sarah was eighty years old and had never had a baby when God told Abraham he would have a son as an heir (see Gen. 15). Everywhere she looked it said that she would be barren her whole life. She couldn't find another eighty-year-old woman who had ever had a baby that would encourage her to believe that God could also do it for her.

10. When you look around, are there examples of other people who birthed a dream similar to yours? What encouragement can you draw in from them? What if you can't find any examples?

....

....

....

....

....

....

God said in effect to eighty-year-old Sarah, "I will give you a son. You will be the mother of nations and kings." Although she was barren, living in the desert, with no medical procedures and no infertility treatments available, God said, "You have kings in you. You have nations in you."

11. How does Sarah's example inspire and encourage you?

....

....

....

....

....

....

....

The prophet Joel said, "Wake up the mighty men!" (Joel 3:9 NKJV). I'm here to wake up your dreams, wake up your talents, wake up your potential, wake up what God put in you. You may have let some circumstances convince you that it's never going to happen, but I believe you're going to start feeling some kicking on the inside. That baby, that dream, that promise is still alive in you. You better get ready.

12. The lady who had had a stroke needed to "fight the good fight of the faith" (1 Tim. 6:12). How does her story speak to you about overcoming life's challenges and setbacks?

....

....

....

....

....

Genesis 3:15 says that the seed of the woman will bruise the head of the serpent, who deceived Eve in the Garden of Eden and brought about all kinds of trouble. God was saying in effect, "Eve, it's payback time. You're going to give birth to something that's going to defeat the thing that's tried to defeat you. Your seed will bruise his head."

13. What has God already put on the inside of you that when birthed will help you overcome and accomplish your dream?

....

....

....

....

....

....

"Well, Joel, I believe I'm pregnant. I have big dreams, and I'm standing on God's promises, but it seems as though the more I pray, the worse it gets. I'm doing the right thing, but the wrong thing is happening." Here's the beauty: Pain is a sign that you're about to give birth. Difficulties, being uncomfortable—those are signs that you're getting closer.

14. Describe the things that are coming against you. How are the pains getting more intense?

....

....

....

....

....

....

15. What did you take away from the wild mushroom and cat story? Are what you consider setbacks merely a part of the birthing process?

....

....

> *Keep doing the right thing. The birth is on the way.*

....

....

....

....

....

....

16. Stephen King had a dream to become a writer but was so discouraged by rejected manuscripts that he was a step away from giving up. What can you draw from his story to encourage you in seeing your dream birthed?

....

....

....

....

....

Keep trying, keep believing, keep doing everything you can, and at the right time you will give birth.

....

....

....

17. You are pregnant with victory, pregnant with success, pregnant with the favor of God. You've had disappointments, but you can still feel the kicking on the inside. Write down the words of faith that you will speak out loud to see everything that God has put in you come to birth.

....

....

....

....

....

....

....

....

CHAPTER SIX

The Promise Is in You

So often, we look at others and think, *Wow, they are so amazing, smart, beautiful, and I am so ordinary.* While it's true that they may be amazing in certain areas, you have to realize there's something amazing about you as well. You have been fearfully and wonderfully made. You didn't get left out when God was handing out the gifts, the talents, or the looks. He put something in you that will cause you to shine. You can be a great businessperson, a great teacher, a great mother. Don't get so focused on what somebody else has that you don't realize what you have.

1. On a scale of 1 to 10, with 1 being a negative view and 10 being a very positive view, how would you say you view yourself? Review why you have given yourself that score.

   ....

   ....

   ....

   ....

   ....

2. What thoughts can you use today to immediately begin to improve your score?

   ....

   ....

   ....

   ....

For many years, I cheered my father on. I'd see my father speaking to thousands of people, making a difference, doing something great. In the back of my mind, I thought, *I could never do that. He's so gifted. He's so talented.* After I came back from college, I worked for seventeen years behind the scenes at the church with my parents, doing the television production and doing my best to make my father look good.

3. Who are the people in your life whom you especially celebrate?

....

....

....

....

....

When my father died, even though I'd never ministered or been to seminary, I heard a still small voice saying, "Joel, you've spent your whole life celebrating others. Now it's time for you to be celebrated and to step up to a new level of your destiny." I always knew that God had promised to take care of the church after my dad was gone, but I never dreamed it would be through me. I discovered *the promise was in me.*

4. What promise has God put in you? What is He saying about your life?

....

....

....

....

....

....

God will never ask you for something without first putting it in you. When God gives you a dream, when you have a desire and you know you're supposed to take a step of faith, you may feel completely unqualified. You may tell yourself that you don't have the wisdom, the know-how, or the ability. But if you'll dare to take that step, just as I did, you'll discover things in you that you never knew you had.

5. What was your immediate response to this life principle? Have you recognized that it is true in your life? In what ways do you, and in what ways have you not?

    ....

    ....

    ....

    ....

> *It's time for you to think better thoughts about yourself. It's time for you to shine.*

....

....

....

....

....

....

....

....

....

....

....

This is where Sarah, Abraham's wife, almost missed it. She had the promise of God, but she thought it would come through somebody else.

6. What promise did God tell Sarah He had put in her, and how did she respond?

....

....

....

....

....

....

....

....

7. Have you responded to a promise God has put in you in a manner similar to Sarah? How did it work out? Have you been able to return to the promise and see it fulfilled as Sarah did?

....

....

....

....

....

....

> *You don't need anyone else to give birth to the promise that God put in your heart.*

....

....

....

Dr. Todd Price grew up very poor. From the time he was a little boy, he had a desire to help children in need. One day he saw a program on television describing how he could sponsor a needy child for fifteen dollars a month. His heart was so moved that he started mowing lawns to raise the money. When he was twelve years old, he started to sponsor his first child. What caused him to do that? It was the promise God put in him. It was a seed of greatness waiting to be developed.

8. As Dr. Price grew up, what was his prayer and passion? What did he do in addition to praying?

....

....

....

....

....

9. What amazing discovery did Dr. Price ultimately make?

....

....

....

....

....

10. Are you waiting for someone else to give birth to what God has placed in your heart? What if you are the answer to your prayers?

....

....

....

....

....

After God gave Sarah the promise of a child, she didn't believe it would happen and made a mess. But God doesn't change His mind. A dozen or so years went by before she finally believed and gave birth to Isaac.

11. What does that say to you about the promises God has placed in you that remain to be birthed?

....

....

....

....

Forty years after the nation of Israel failed to go into the Promised Land, Caleb was eighty-five years old and still fired up to conquer their enemies. He knew the promise was still in him.

12. Does one's age or mistakes made along the way excuse us from fulfilling the promises God has put in us? Why or why not?

....

....

....

....

13. Caleb conquered a mountain on which he knew three giants lived. What does that say about the opposition to your fulfilling the promises?

....

....

....

....

....

When a gazelle or a wildebeest is pregnant and about to give birth, a lion will closely stalk that animal, waiting for her to go into labor. The lion knows that when she goes into labor, she's an easy target, because she can't defend herself or her baby against its attack.

14. You will face your greatest attacks when you're about to give birth to the dreams God placed in your heart. How can you prepare yourself to overcome whatever the enemy brings your way?

....

....

....

....

....

....

15. Reread the story about the young man named Troy. Despite the bleakest of circumstances, he had a big dream for his life. What did he do to help bring it to pass that you can also do to see your dream fulfilled?

....

....

....

....

....

....

....

....

....

....

In the Scripture, God put a promise in Jeremiah that he would be a prophet and speak to the nations, but people and obstacles came against him. He got so discouraged that he was about to give up. Jeremiah began to list one complaint after another. But just when you thought Jeremiah was going to quit, he said, "[God, Your] word is in my heart like a fire, a fire shut up in my bones" (Jer. 20:9). He was saying, "God, I don't see how it can happen. But this promise You put in me will not go away. It's like fire. It's like a burning. I can't get away from it." When Jeremiah began to think better and let the fire burn, his life passion was restored.

16. Each of us faces times of discouragement about fulfilling what God has put in our heart. What can you draw from Jeremiah's confession to help you accomplish more than you ever dreamed possible?

> *You are equipped. You are anointed. You are the right person. You have what it takes. It's time for you to do something great!*

....

....

....

....

....

....

....

....

....

....

....

....

....

CHAPTER SEVEN

Ask Big

When God laid out the plan for your life, He didn't just put into it what you need to get by to survive. He put more than enough in it. He's a God of abundance. We see this all throughout the Scripture. After Jesus multiplied the little boy's five loaves of bread and two fish, thousands of people ate, and yet there were twelve basketfuls of leftovers (see John 6:13). He could have made just enough so there would be no leftovers. On purpose, He made more than enough. That's the God we serve.

1. David said, "My cup overflows" (Ps. 23:5). He had an abundance, more than he needed. What is your first reaction to the statement that God is a God of abundance? Do you have an abundance mentality?

....

....

....

> God wants you to have an abundance, so you can be a blessing to those around you.

....

....

....

....

....

....

....

....

....

The Israelites had been in slavery for so many years that they became conditioned to not having enough, to barely getting by. When Pharaoh demanded that they make the same amount of bricks without the straw being provided for them, I'm sure the Israelites prayed, "God, please help us to find the supplies that we need and to make our quotas."

2. What does it mean to pray with a slave mentality? What should they have been praying for?

....

....

....

....

....

....

3. If someone were to evaluate your prayers, would they say you pray with a slave mentality or an abundant mentality? Elaborate on that.

....

....

....

....

....

....

....

....

....

Are you asking today to become a better slave or are you asking for the abundant, overflowing, more-than-enough life that God has for you? God says you are to reign in life, that you are blessed and you cannot be cursed, that whatever you touch will prosper and succeed. Don't pray to just get by, to endure. Dare to ask big.

4. Name an area of your prayer life you want to change to a prayer of abundance. What has your prayer been, and what are you changing it to?

....

> *Ask God for what He has promised you in His Word.*

....

....

....

....

....

5. Write out several promises in God's Word that you can incorporate into your thoughts that will help you to pray big.

....

....

....

....

....

....

....

....

....

In the story of the grandmother who ended up raising her four small grandchildren, she had the boldness to ask big. She said, "God, I don't have the funds to keep my grandchildren in private school, but I know You own it all. You're a God of abundance. And, God, I'm asking You to make a way, even though I don't see how it can ever happen."

6. What would her prayer have been if she had a slave mentality?

....

....

....

....

7. What did God make happen because she didn't have a limited mind-set?

....

....

....

....

8. My question is, "Are you asking big?" How does your thinking need to change to get to abundance in all areas of your life?

....

....

....

....

....

....

Matthew 20 records the story of Jesus walking through a town where there were two blind men who started shouting, "Jesus, have mercy on us!" Jesus asked them, "What do you want me to do for you?" (v. 32). It seemed like a strange question to ask men whose need was so obvious.

9. Why did Jesus ask them what they wanted Him to do for them?

....

....

....

....

....

....

10. If Jesus were to ask you the same thing he asked those two blind men, how would you answer? (He is asking you that, by the way, and how you answer is going to have a great impact on what God does.)

....

....

....

> *Do what the blind men did. Dare to ask big. Dare to ask even for what seems impossible.*

....

....

....

....

....

....

In 1 Chronicles 4, there was a man by the name of Jabez, which literally means "pain, sorrow, suffering." Every time someone called his name, they were saying "Hello, sorrow and pain." They were prophesying defeat and failure and making him feel inferior and insecure. Despite what people labeled him, Jabez prayed, "God, bless me and enlarge my territory." He had the boldness to ask big, "and God granted his request."

11. What was it about Jabez's attitude that helped him to shake off the slave mentality and the negatives that people had put on him?

....

....

....

....

....

....

12. Like Jabez, you may have plenty of reasons to settle where you are—what you didn't get, what people said, how impossible it looks. What good news from God will keep you from praying weak, sick prayers?

....

....

....

....

....

....

....

God said in Psalm 2 MSG, "You're my son, and today is your birthday. What do you want? Name it: Nations as a present? Continents as a prize? You can command them all to dance for you." Notice how big God thinks. We're praying for a promotion; God's talking about giving you nations. We're praying to pay our bills; God's planning on blessing you so you can pay other people's bills. We're looking at the five loaves and two fish; God's thinking about the twelve basketfuls of leftovers.

13. What does "Today is your birthday" mean to you in a general sense?

....

....

....

14. What does "Today is your birthday" mean to you when God says it?

....

....

....

....

15. What difference would it make if you approached every new day with the belief that God has made it your birthday?

....

....

....

....

....

Too often, instead of approaching God as though it's our birthday, believing that He'll do something special, we do just the opposite. "I can't ask for what I really want. That would be selfish." Jesus said, "...it is your Father's good pleasure to give you the kingdom" (Luke 12:32 NKJV). Nothing makes God happier than for Him to see you step up to who you were created to be.

16. What was your immediate response to Jesus' statement about our Father in Heaven? Is that how you come to Him in prayer and in life? Describe who He is and how He looks upon you as His child.

> *God will move heaven and earth to bring about His destiny in your life.*

17. Are there limits to what God says you can ask for in prayer? Does the word *impossible* pertain to what God can do?

18. In Psalm 72, Solomon prayed what seemed to be a very self-centered prayer. What did he ask God for? How would you have thought God would answer him?

....

....

....

....

....

....

19. Why did God answer Solomon's big bold prayer with a yes?

....

....

....

....

....

20. God is raising up a new generation of Solomons, people who have the boldness to ask God to make them influential with gifts and talents that stand out. Join them and write a big bold prayer to that effect for your life as well.

....

....

....

....

....

....

CHAPTER EIGHT

You Have What You Need

So often we think, *If I had more money, I could accomplish my dreams. If I had a bigger house, I'd be happy. If I had more talent, I could do something great.* But as long as you feel as though you're lacking or were shortchanged, you'll make excuses to be less than your best.

You have to get a new perspective. God has given you exactly what you need for the season you're in. You have the talent, the friends, the connections, the resources, and the experience you need for right now.

1. Psalm 34:10 says, "Those who seek the LORD lack no good thing." Describe what that means.

   ....

   ....

   ....

   ....

   ....

2. Do you believe that for the season of life you are now in that you have exactly what you need? Write down your immediate response.

   ....

   ....

   ....

   ....

   ....

   ....

Several years ago, someone published an article that talked about how I haven't been to seminary and how I wasn't qualified to lead a large ministry. At first that bothered me. Then I read Galatians 1:1, where the apostle Paul, who wrote about half the books of the New Testament, said that his calling to preach the gospel was "not from men nor by a man, but by Jesus Christ and God the Father, who raised him from the dead."

3. What if people do not approve of you in the plan that you feel God has given for your life? How do you respond to their disapproval?

> *Don't let what some person says or does make you feel less than or unqualified.*

4. What changes can you make in what you tell yourself that will empower you to live not feeling you are lacking or short-changed?

Second Samuel 12 tells the story of how King David got off course with his life. The prophet Nathan was correcting him. In doing so, he reminded David that he had experienced God's goodness, favor, protection, provision, and healing down through the years. God made an interesting statement through Nathan: "David, if it had not been enough, I would have given you much, much more" (v. 8 NLT).

5. What does that tell you about what you need to fulfill your destiny?

....

....

....

....

....

....

....

6. Describe one area of your life that you will start to apply this truth to immediately.

....

....

....

....

....

....

....

7. When my father started Lakewood with ninety people in an old feed store, his future did not look so bright and he could have been very disheartened. What could he have thought, and what did he think instead?

....

....

....

....

....

....

Jesus met a Samaritan woman at a well and gave her the amazing promise that if she asked Him, He would give her living water that would cause her to never thirst again. However, she immediately began to view His promise from her very limited human perspective.

8. Has God put a promise in your heart, but you've been talking yourself out of it with negative thoughts about what you don't have? What promise has God put in you, and what better thoughts will help bring it to pass?

....

....

God knows what you need and when you need it, and He knows how to get it to you.

....

....

....

....

....

....

....

....

All David had was a slingshot and five smooth stones when he defeated Goliath. All Samson had was the jawbone of a donkey when he defeated an entire army of a thousand men. All Moses had was an ordinary stick that he held in the air and the Red Sea supernaturally parted.

9. What do you have? What has God given you? Do you underestimate what He has given you and the person He is calling you to be?

....

....

....

....

....

....

....

10. Zechariah 4:10 says, "Do not despise these small beginnings." What is it that seems small and insignificant in your life now that God wants to breathe upon and turn into so much more?

....

....

....

....

....

....

....

On one occasion, Jesus had been teaching thousands of people. It was late in the day when Jesus turned to His disciples and said, "I want you to feed all these people." They didn't have any food out there in the wilderness. There were no grocery stores. On the surface, it seemed as though what Jesus asked was impossible. But here's the key: God will never ask you to do something and then not give you the ability to do it.

11. What was your immediate reaction to this key statement? Did you agree with it or have reservations? Why?

....

....

....

....

....

....

....

12. Jesus took the five loaves and the two fish, prayed over them, and they supernaturally multiplied. What does that say to you about an "I don't have enough" mentality?

....

....

....

....

....

....

....

....

....

13. Mary Bethune had a dream to teach young people but seemingly had nothing of what she needed to start her own school. What did she have? How does her pathway to fulfilling her dream compare to yours?

> *Mary Bethune was the first African-American woman to become a presidential advisor.*

The Scripture tells of four starving lepers who were marching toward an enemy's camp. God multiplied the sound of their footsteps to sound like a huge army was attacking. Their enemies ran away and left their food behind, saving the lepers' lives and the people of Samaria as well.

14. The lepers had nothing but their footsteps. What do you have? How does what they had compare to what you have as regards the fulfilling of your dream?

When David prepared to face Goliath without any armor, King Saul tried to get David to wear his armor. However, David was much smaller than King Saul, and the armor swallowed him. It would have only slowed him down because it didn't fit. All he needed was his slingshot.

15. Have you ever tried to be like or copy someone else? Describe your experience. Why does it never work to wear someone else's armor?

_____

_____

_____

_____

_____

_____

_____

_____

16. Goliath was wearing a full set of armor and had a huge spear. All David had was the slingshot. What was the difference? What will make the difference in your life battles?

_____

_____

_____

_____

_____

_____

A few years ago I was speaking to several hundred pastors. Afterward we had a time for questions. One pastor who stood up was a very large man, about six feet five inches tall and three hundred pounds. I am five feet nine inches tall. He said very dramatically, "Joel, I just want to know, how much do you weigh?" I smiled and said, "I'm one hundred and fifty pounds of pure steel!"

17. What thoughts can you use to improve your confidence in who God made you to be?

   ....

   ....

   ....

   ....

   ....

   ....

18. Write a statement of faith declaring what God has given you, then copy it on another sheet of paper and place it on your bathroom mirror and repeat it out loud every morning.

   ....

   ....

   ....

   ....

   ....

   ....

   ....

   ....

CHAPTER NINE

Keep Your Crown

When God breathed His life into you, He put "a crown of glory and honor" on your head. This crown represents your authority. It represents God's blessing and favor on your life. It's a reminder that you're not average, you're not mediocre: You are royalty. When you're wearing your crown, you'll have a sense of entitlement, thinking, *I have a right to be blessed. I have a right to live in victory. I have a right to overcome these challenges—not because I'm so great or so talented, but because I'm wearing a crown of honor put there by my Creator.*

1. Your perception of yourself will determine what kind of life you live. On a scale of 1 to 10, with 1 being less than average and 10 being royalty, how would you grade yourself? Describe your perception of yourself.

....

....

....

> "You have made them a little lower than the angels and crowned them with glory and honor."
> PSALM 8:5

....

....

....

....

....

....

....

Jesus said, "Hold on to what you have, so that no one will take your crown" (Rev. 3:11). Throughout life, there will always be someone or something trying to take your crown. People will talk about you, trying to make you look bad, to push you down. What they're really doing is trying to get your crown.

2. What have people said or what thoughts do you have that try to get your crown?

> *"No one can make you feel inferior without your permission."*
> ELEANOR ROOSEVELT

....

....

....

....

....

....

....

....

3. What better thoughts will counter those negative words or thoughts?

....

....

....

....

....

....

....

....

After you've written your better thoughts, speak them out loud and declare that nothing can take your crown from you.

When somebody tries to make you feel small, they make derogatory statements. Instead of being upset, just reach up and straighten your crown. That's why God put the crown of honor on your head. It's to remind you of who you are. They can't change who you are unless you allow them to. They don't control your destiny or determine your value. They didn't breathe life into you; God did. He calls you a masterpiece. He says you're a king, a queen. You're supposed to reign in life.

4. What is the enemy's main tool, and what mistake do we too often make in our thoughts about our circumstances and what people say?

....

....

....

....

....

....

5. What did the baseball coach fail to see in the young man whom he thought was too small to make the team? How does the young man's example encourage you to keep your crown on at all times?

....

....

....

....

....

....

....

Jesus said to His critics, "Your approval means nothing to Me" (John 5:41 NLT). That's a powerful way to live. He was saying, "I know who I am, and nothing you do or don't do is going to change Me. You can celebrate Me or you can crucify Me, but I'm keeping My crown."

6. What was your immediate response to Jesus' statement? Write an honest review of how much other people's approval or disapproval of you affects the way you live.

....

....

....

....

....

....

....

7. What is the problem with needing other people's approval? What better thoughts will keep you free from others carrying away your blessing?

....

....

....

....

....

....

....

The enemy has been trying to get our crown from the beginning of time. In the Garden of Eden, Adam and Eve were living confident and secure, at peace with God, at peace with themselves. They were wearing their crowns. But one day the enemy deceived them into eating the forbidden fruit. When they did, immediately they were afraid. They ran and hid. In effect, they gave the enemy their crowns.

8. What happens when you surrender your crown of honor? Describe it.

> *Where there's no crown, there's no covering.*

....

....

....

....

....

....

When God came looking for Adam and Eve, He asked, "Who told you that you were naked?" And He is asking us today, "Who told you that there's something wrong with you? Who told you that you're just average? That you can't accomplish your dreams? That you're not good enough?"

9. Identify the source of these lies and write out the thoughts that will help you take back your crown and keep it on.

....

....

....

....

....

....

....

The beautiful young lady whose husband left her for someone else was also left with the feeling it was all her fault, that she had failed. And she was convinced that she wasn't attractive enough, talented enough, or smart enough. She had given her crown away.

10. Perhaps you've been through the disappointment of a relationship that didn't work out. Perhaps you're going through one now. What has the accuser been trying to convince you about your role in it?

....

....

....

....

....

....

....

11. What powerful thoughts will defeat the accuser's lies when you face disappointment and loss in a relationship and help keep your crown on?

....

....

....

....

....

....

....

In the Scripture, a woman named Naomi first lost her husband, then both her married sons died as well. She was so discouraged that she didn't think she could go on. She even changed her name from Naomi, which means "my joy," to Mara, which means "bitter." She was saying, "Call me bitter," but some of her old friends refused and kept calling her, "My joy." They kept putting her crown back on.

12. Do you have friends in your life who remind you about who you are, who encourage and bless you? What can you do to develop a deeper relationship with them?

....

....

....

....

....

....

13. Naomi thought she'd never be happy again, but after the birth of Ruth's son, she was more fulfilled than ever. What does that tell you about keeping your crown on during periods of difficulty and challenge?

....

....

....

....

....

....

....

In the mythological story about Helen of Troy, she had royalty in her blood but had somehow forgotten who she was. She had to rediscover who she was and become the queen she was always meant to be. Young Prince Louis XVII, on the other hand, was subjected to great pressure to reprogram his thinking and abdicate his right as the royal heir.

14. You are a child of the Most High God, crowned with honor and glory. Do you struggle with forgetting who you are, or do you feel the pressure to reprogram your thinking to be less than a king or queen? Write out power thoughts for how you will keep your crown on, no matter what life brings.

....

....

....

....

....

....

....

....

> *The chains of defeated thinking and a negative mentality are being loosened. Strongholds that have held you back are being broken.*

....

....

....

....

....

CHAPTER TEN

Just Remember

When you look back over your life, consider some of the things you've faced that at the time you didn't think you could make it through. The obstacle was so large, the breakup hurt you so badly, the medical report was so negative. You didn't see a way, but God turned it around. He gave you strength when you didn't think you could go on. That wasn't a lucky break. It wasn't a coincidence. It was the hand of God.

1. Describe a past event or circumstance where God made a way for you when there was no way. How does that build faith in your heart for whatever you're facing today or will face in the future?

> *Remember that God is taking you from glory to glory.*

When the Israelites came out of slavery in Egypt with no military training or weapons, God said to them in Deuteronomy 7, "You may think, 'How can we conquer these nations that are much stronger than us?' But don't be afraid. Just remember what I did to Pharaoh. You saw the miraculous signs and power I used to bring you out." God was saying, "When it looks impossible, the way to stay encouraged and keep your hopes up is to remember what God has done."

2. As you did with question 1, describe another time when you saw God open a door or answer a prayer when your dream looked impossible.

....

....

....

....

....

....

....

....

3. Write a declaration of faith that states and reminds you of the fact that God is in control of your life and directing your steps.

....

....

....

....

....

When the apostle Paul talks about "the mercies of God" in Romans 12:1, he doesn't use the singular but the plural. Every one of us has experienced some of these mercies. For me, the many mercies of God have been represented in my walking into the jewelry store and meeting Victoria as well as being spared from an accident with an eighteen-wheeler when I lost control of my car during a rainstorm.

4. Describe a time or incident in your life when you experienced the mercies of God.

_____

_____

_____

_____

_____

_____

_____

5. Based on the mercies of God, Paul adds that we should dedicate all of ourselves to Him as "a living sacrifice." What wonderful things happen when we surrender our will to His?

_____

_____

_____

_____

_____

_____

_____

David said, "If the LORD had not been on our side...the raging waters would have swept us away" (Ps. 124:1–4). He was saying in effect, "If God had not shown me some of His mercies, I wouldn't have defeated Goliath, outlasted King Saul when he was trying to kill me, or been restored after my sin with Bathsheba."

6. The psalmist says, "My enemies have never been able to finish me off!" (Ps. 129:2 TLB). What is it in your life that the enemy has tried to but has not been able to finish you off because the Lord has been on your side?

....

....

....

....

Sometimes you need to just thank God that you're still here.

....

....

....

....

....

7. God has the final say in our lives. What truth will you declare when the enemy comes against you?

....

....

....

....

....

God is called "the author and the finisher of our faith" (Heb. 12:1 NKJV). What He started in your life, He will finish—not a bad break, not a disappointment, not a sickness. God is the finisher. In the New Testament days, Saul was one of the greatest enemies of the church. He was headed to Damascus to persecute believers who didn't even know he was coming. It looked inevitable. But suddenly a bright light shone down on Saul from Heaven. In a split second, God stopped the persecutor in his tracks...and in the process changed him into an apostle.

8. What does it mean that God is the finisher of your faith? What about all the things that you have no control over and aren't even aware of that are coming against you?

....

....

....

....

....

....

9. What about your bad breaks and disappointments? What do you need to quit thinking about them?

....

....

....

....

....

....

David said in Psalm 34, "Let all who are discouraged take heart."
He goes on to tell us how to do it. "Come, let's talk about God's
goodness. I prayed and the Lord answered my prayer." He was saying, "When you're discouraged, when you don't see a way out, come
and let's talk about God's greatness. Let's talk about your answered
prayers."

10. Start remembering your victories, the times God healed you,
promoted you, turned the problems around. Write down three
specific victories that God has worked in your life and what you
want people to know about how God did them.

*Don't let what
once was a miracle
become ordinary.
Don't lose the awe
of what God
has done.*

I must have heard my father tell the story a thousand times of how he gave his life to Christ. It happened when he was seventeen, but at seventy-five years old he was still telling it as though it happened just yesterday. He never lost the amazement.

11. When you constantly think about what God has done, when you relive your miracles, when you're always in awe of His goodness, what do you put yourself in position for?

12. Describe one thing that God has done in your life that always amazes you and makes you want to tell others about it.

Just a few hours after the disciples had seen with their own eyes one of the greatest miracles ever recorded, they were caught in a nighttime storm on a lake, fearful for their lives, and terrified when Jesus came to them walking on the waters in the dark (see Mark 6). When He got into the boat, the winds and waves calmed down immediately. The Scripture tells us they were so worried because "they still didn't understand the significance of the miracle of the loaves" (v. 52 NLT).

13. What would have happened if the disciples had just remembered the miracle?

_____

_____

_____

All the forces of darkness cannot hold you back.

_____

_____

_____

14. Are you allowing your circumstances, a medical report, or a financial situation to cause you to live worried, stressed out? What better thoughts of remembrance will cause you to rise up and accomplish your dreams?

_____

_____

_____

_____

_____

_____

STAY**CONNECTED,**
BE**BLESSED.**

From thoughtful articles to powerful blogs, podcasts and more, JoelOsteen.com is full of inspirations that will give you encouragement and confidence in your daily life.

AVAILABLE ON JOELOSTEEN.COM

This daily devotional from Joel and Victoria will help you grow in your relationship with the Lord and equip you to be everything God intends you to be.

Joel Osteen
STREAMING

Miss a broadcast? Watch Joel Osteen on demand, and see Joel LIVE on Sundays.

Joel Osteen
PODCAST

The podcast is a great way to listen to Joel where you want, when you want.

CONNECT WITH US

Join our community of believers on your favorite social network.

TAKE HOPE WITH YOU

Get the inspiration and encouragement of Joel Osteen on your iPhone, iPad or Android device! Our app puts Joel's messages, devotions and more at your fingertips.

Thanks for helping us make a difference in the lives of millions around the world.